AFRICAN AMERICAN BAPTIST IN MISSION: A HISTORICAL GUIDE

Highlighting National Baptist Convention USA, Inc. Foreign Mission Board mission ministry and mission leadership until 2007

BY

REV. DR. ROXANNE JONES BOOTH

Endorsements: African American Baptist in Mission: A Historical Guide

Roxanne Jones Booth makes an important contribution to the studies of global missions, African-American history, and the witness of the National Baptist Convention, USA, Inc. Foreign Mission Board. Her missionary service in Southern Africa, academic training in missions, teaching experience in higher education, and vocation as a pastor give her a unique perspective to inform and interpret this rich heritage for new generations of learners and leaders.

David Emmanuel Goatley
Lott Carey Baptist Foreign Mission Convention
Washington, DC

This is a marvelous book that not only fills a gap in mission history based on solid research, but will also provoke the 21st century African American Baptist church to pick up and run with the mandate of the Great Commission. I am greatly impressed by the emphasis Dr. Booth gives to the fearless and unwavering determination of our missionary forerunners.

Rev. Victor E. Covington
Pastor of the Union Missionary Baptist Church
Albany, New York

The writing of Rev. Dr. Roxanne Jones Booth not only unquestionably reminds the reader of the founding purpose of our national body, but it celebrates the continuous, unwavering, sacrificial work of African Americans to spread the message of the gospel of Jesus Christ. To our detriment, few congregants have received the education of our rich history of international missions. Dr. Booth's writing provides a history which can be a launching pad for a wide array of African Americans serving in 21st century global missions.

Reverend Cassandra Aline Jones, PhD
Professor of Christian Education
Chair, General Studies Department
Charlotte Christian College and Theological Seminary
Charlotte, North Carolina

Table of Contents

Introduction

*T*his historical guide of African American Baptist in mission was motivated out of the need to fill a gap in mission history in the United States of America which typically begins with Adoniram Judson's ministry in Burma in the early 1800's. Mission history, as taught in the United States of America, has yet to acknowledge George Liele an enslaved African who purchased his freedom and became the first *American* to leave the shores of the continental USA to share the message of Jesus Christ cross-culturally. Liele, the first *American* missionary, established Baptist Churches in Jamaica in 1782.

Much of the history of the African American Baptists' work in mission has been preserved in documents such as the *Mission Herald*, the periodical of the National Baptist Convention USA, Inc. Foreign Mission Board (FMB) established in 1895. This periodical was first published in the early 1900's to document the mission activities of the largest African American religious body in the United States of America.

The FMB has been involved in international mission ministry since 1897. Its focus initially was Africa. In the early years, 1897 to 1910, the FMB sent up to 15 mission workers to Africa. Over the years not only were African American mission workers sent to Africa, but Africans were also brought to the United States of America by the FMB to be educated before returning to Africa to carry on ministry in their homeland. Mission workers of the FMB have included African nationals as mission workers in the past and continue to do so today.

This historical guide will highlight the mission interest of African American Baptists through the mission administration leadership of the FMB. The administrative leadership of the mission ministry of the FMB is through the office of the Corresponding Secretary, which later is called the Executive Secretary. Each administration of the

FMB carried out specific and innovative mission ministry activities which expanded its work both home and aboard.

Dedication:

I thank God for blessing me with a wonderful, God-
loving husband who is my greatest supporter and the
one who keeps me motivated.
Rev. Antonio Booth, thank you for loving me, always.
I dedicate this book to you.

Acknowledgements:

To God be the glory; great things God has done!
I would like to acknowledge the great people of the
National Baptist Churches of Swaziland who allowed
me to minister with them as their pastor for two years
and mission worker for five years following my grad-
uation from seminary and who graciously accepted my
husband and me as ministry leaders for three years.
Swaziland is where I cut my teeth in ministry. It will
always hold a special place in my heart.
I would also like acknowledge the wonderful people of
the African United National Baptist Churches in South
Africa where I was allowed to come alongside church
leaders and establish a ministry for young people that
has developed into the your Annual Youth Conference.

Lastly, I would like to acknowledge a few people of
Riverview Missionary Baptist Church and the Hamlet
of Coeymans who where my "copy editors."
I would like to especially thank Dave and Starr Ross,
Deana Ferrusi and Pastor Antonio Booth
for your editorial gifting.

Look what God has done!

AFRICAN AMERICANS AND MISSION MINISTRY

discussion of the formation of the African American Baptist in mission begins on the shores of West Africa. The story begins with Africans huddled in small cramped holding pens, confused, bewildered and tormented by unrelenting slave traders. They have been forcibly removed from their families and land to be sold in the Trans-Atlantic Slave Trade. Surviving the "Middle Passage," the Africans arrive in the Americas stripped of personhood and dignity and clinging only to their faith.

In spite of their degrading and dehumanizing transport to the new world, enslaved Africans arrived in the Americas with religious convictions representative of the traditional beliefs and customs of the countries of their origin. In their book, *The Black Church in the African American Experience*, C. Eric Lincoln and Lawrence H. Mamiya discuss the vestiges of African traditional beliefs that survived the "Middle passage." These authors draw our attention to what they term, "The Black Sacred Cosmos"[1] This religious worldview of African Americans, they contend, "is related both to their African heritage, which envisages the whole universe as sacred, and their conversion to Christianity during slavery and its aftermath."[2] They further state that "black people created their own unique and distinctive forms of culture in which they were involuntary guests."[3]

Documented in an article written by this author in the *Journal of Constructive Theology*, Lincoln and Mamiya discuss the extent to which African culture was transplanted and preserved in the United States.[4]

---

[1] C. Eric Lincoln and Lawrence H. Mamiya, *The Black Church in the African American Experience* (Durham and London: Duke University Press, 1990), 2-5.

[2] Ibid, 2.

[3] Ibid, 2.

[4] For a closer discussion on African survivals read John Hope Franklin, From Slavery to Freedom: A History of Negro Americans (New York: Alfred A. Knopf, Inc.,1980), 28-29.

The debate still ensues as to whether Africans continued to be African except in color and whether any African cultural distinctions became a part of their condition of slavery in the United States. Researchers like Carter G. Woodson, Melville J. Herskovits and Lorenzo Turner have insisted that African cultural distinctions can still be seen in many aspects of African American life today.[5]

Enslaved Africans with their traditional religious beliefs met Christianity in slavery and forged for themselves a religious understanding that reflected the totality of their condition in the United States of America.[6]

Albert Raboteau in his book, *Slave Religion: The Invisible Institution in the Ante-bellum South,* discusses the unique Christianity that emerged in slave culture in the United States. Slave religion was that religion that was able to adapt the religion of the oppressor.[7]

---

[5] Roxanne Jones, "African American Religious Influence in South Africa: The Case of the Baptist Church," Journal of Constructive Theology Vol. 4, No. 2 (December 1998):88.

[6] Ibid, 89.

[7] Albert Raboteau, *Slave Religion: The "Invisible Church" in the Antebellum South* (Oxford: oxford University Press, 1978), 92.

While in bondage the African slave held on to the basic emphasis of Christianity which was a respect for human personality. Jesus taught that persons are children of God and the Kingdom of God is in each person. This obliges all to treat others in Christ not as objects, but as subject-centers of high value and worth. The slave found in the religion of Jesus an interpretation of the relation of humankind to God which inspired the imagination and gave hope for a future in which the justice of God would ultimately prevail. So they adapted the Christianity they were taught and shaped it into their unique spiritual needs. They believed in the eternal goodness of God, but concluded that 'evebody talkin' 'bout hev'en ain't goin'ther.[8]

No doubt the African American religious experience in the United States is unique and dynamic. Brought to the new world as slaves, Africans were regarded as property. Enslaved Africans were nothing more than a commodity to be bought and sold. Yet, it is in spite of these beginnings and also because of them that the call of the "Great Commission" was heard and heeded among the enslaved. Lott Carey, the first African American (Baptist)

---

[8] Ibid, 89.

missionary sent to Liberia in 1820, when asked why he would leave the comforts of home to travel to Africa to evangelize, stated,

> I am an African, and in this Country, however meritorious my conduct and respectable my character, I cannot receive the credit due to either. I wish to go to a country where I shall be estimated by my merits not by my complexion; and I feel bound to labor for my suffering race.[9]

After the US Civil War emigration to Africa was the hope of many newly freed Africans in America. Gayraud S. Wilmore in his article, "Black Americans in Missions: Setting the Record Straight" documents that as early as 1878, only 13 years after the US Civil War, 200 African Americans organized the Liberian Exodus Joint Stock Steamship Company and sailed for Liberia believing that "African emigration was the only possibility of survival."[10] Two African American Baptist preachers went with

---

[9] Leroy Fitts, *Lott Carey: First Black Missionary to Africa* (Valley Forge, PA: Judson Press, 1982), 18-19.

[10] Gayraud S. Wilmore, "Black Americans in Mission: Setting the Record Straight," International Bulletin of Missionary Research (July 1986): 99.

this contingency. Wilmore suggests that this was the first postwar bid to establish an African American missionary presence in Africa.[11] The focus of these developments will be discussed in a later section of this chapter.

---

[11] Ibid, 100.

ENSLAVED AFRICANS AND CHRISTIANITY

Following the Great Awakenings of the late 18th and early 19th Centuries, enslaved Africans were brought into the folds of the Baptists and Methodist churches.[12] However, Christianity was not introduced to the enslaved without objection. Many enslavers objected to enslaved Africans being evangelized and instructed in Christianity by missionaries of the North. The enslavers believed enslaved Africans were "too brutish to be instructed and incapable of instruction."[13] The more con-

---

[12] Sandy D. Martin, Black Baptists and African Missions: The Origins of a Movement, 1880-1915 (Macon Georgia: Mercer University Press, 1989), 7.

[13] Raboteau, 100

troversial issue with regard to slave evangelism was the question of what would be the enslaved condition of servitude after converting to Christianity. Raboteau states from a quote taken from John Barbot in *Descriptions of Guinea,*

> One of the principal reasons for the refusal of English planters to allow their slaves to receive instructions was the fear that baptism would emancipate their slaves. The notion that if slaves were baptized, 'they should, according to the laws of the British nations, and the canons of the church' be freed was legally vague but widely believed.[14]

The condition of the enslaved, after conversion, presented a dilemma for the enslaver. Most troubling for enslavers was that Christianity lifted up the ideals of freedom, equality and new life. The enslaver never envisioned these ideas for their property. Lincoln and Mamiya contend that during slavery, *freedom*

> meant release from bondage; after emancipations it meant the right to be educated, to be employed, and to move freely from place. In the twentieth

---

[14] Raboteau, 98.

century freedom means social, political and economic justice. From the very beginning of the
black experience in America, one critical denota-
tion of freedom has remained constant: freedom
has always meant the absence of any restraint
which might compromise one's responsibility
to God.[15]

The last thing the enslaver wanted was for enslaved
Africans to think that being Christian would make them
equal to White folks. Raboteau states that "the most
serious obstacle to the missionary's success to the slaves
was the slaveholder's vague awareness that a Christian
slave would have some claim to fellowship, a claim that
threatened the security of the master-slave hierarchy."[16]

As a result of these attitudes, enslavers imposed
restrictions and regulations on enslaved Africans as
they attempted to follow their newfound faith. Enslaved
Africans were only permitted to attend White Baptist
churches with their master's permission and, only with
written permission were they allowed to leave plantations

[15] Lincoln and Mamiya, 4.
[16] Raboteau, 102.

to attend church where a White clergyman was preaching or attend church under White slave holder supervision.[17]

Debates pursued among enslavers as to the benefit of slaves conversions. Missionaries who advocated for the evangelization of the enslaved argued that "converted slaves do better for their master's profit as they are taught to serve out of Christian Love and Duty."[18] Sermons were preached in the White Baptist churches that emphasized enslaved African's obedience to their masters. Enslavers saw slavery as saving grace for the African. "From the very beginning of the Trans-Atlantic Slave Trade, conversion of the slaves to Christianity was viewed by the emerging nations of Western Christiandom as a justification for enslavement of Africans."[19] These nations viewed African slavery as "the grace of faith made available to Africans, who otherwise would die pagans." [20]

Increasingly, Plantation Missions (churches) were established as enslavers accepted the benefit of enslaved

---

[17] Lincoln and Mamiya, 24.
[18] Raboteau, 103.
[19] Raboteau, 96.
[20] Raboteau, 96.

Africans' conversions. At Plantation Missions African preachers and freed African preachers took up the missionary mantle and were allowed to preach from plantation to plantation under the supervision of White clergymen. The Plantation missions accommodated the large numbers of enslaved Africans that were becoming Christian and consequently outnumbering the Whites in their churches. Missionaries from White churches were assigned to supervise these missions and "devote at least part-time energy to improving religious conditions for slaves."[21]

---

[21] Raboteau, 153.

INDEPENDENT AFRICAN AMERICAN CHURCHES, ASSOCIATIONS AND COOPERATIVES

*T*he seedlings of the independent African American Baptist Church movement grew out of the Plantation Missions. Gradually the message of freedom taught and preached by our Lord and Savior Jesus Christ took hold of the minds and hearts of the enslaved in a new and creative ways; the enslaved "discovered in the Fatherhood of God and the brotherhood of Man a new anthropological concept of human freedom and dignity."[22] To express their Christian faith in their

---

[22] Fitts, 44.

own unique way, free from the watchful eye of Whites, the enslaved met secretly in the early hours of the morning or late at night. It was here in the "hush harbors" that the African American Church was conceived. Fitts states in *History of the Black Baptist,*

> Separate churches could not have been born during slavery if nobody had become dissatisfied with their religious experiences in white churches. The nature of this dissatisfaction may be seen in the necessary response of a Christian conscience to its own enslavement. Central to any independent movement is the prior emergence of free thought.[23]

The pioneer African American missionary and preacher who is credited with establishing the first independent African American Baptist Church was George Liele. In fact, George Liele was the first American missionary to leave the shores of the then colonial United States to share the Gospel of Jesus Christ in foreign lands. Liele was converted while enslaved under the preaching of a White Baptist minister around 1773. A few

---

[23] Fitts, 44.

years after his conversion he organized the first African (American) Baptist Church in Savannah, Georgia. By the 1793 that congregation had out grown its church structure and moved to Augusta, Georgia and formed the First African Baptist Church. Nearly 29 years before Adoniram Judson sailed to Burma Liele sailed to Jamaica with four other freed Africans from the United States in 1784. Liele organized the first Baptist Church in Kingston in 1785.[24] Andrew Byran an enslaved African who had been baptized by Liele organized the First African Baptist Church in Savannah, George in 1788.[25]

The independent church movement grew rapidly in the south with White congregations electing to allow African American members to form their own churches. These same White congregations, however, monitored the activities of the African American churches and only allowed them to make decisions upon their approval.[26] By 1847 there were independent African American Baptist

---

[24] Raboteau, 140.
[25] Lincoln and Mamiya, 24.
[26] Raboteau, 143.

Churches in Massachusetts, Rhode Island, New York City, Brooklyn, New York and Philadelphia.[27] In the north and the south, Lincoln and Mamiya note that the movement for separate churches was against unequal and restrictive practices.[28]

Once African Americans were allowed to form their own churches, cooperatives and associations followed. Fitts notes that "after emancipation, free blacks of the North and South were able to accelerate the organization of churches and develop a cooperative movement among churches."[29] These cooperatives and associations grew rapidly from 1865 to 1961. It is significant to note that when the Baptists split in 1845 over the issue of slavery, the first African American Baptist Church cooperative had already been in existence for thirty years.

The African Baptist Foreign Missionary Society was the first missionary society established by African Americans which constituted a cooperative. Founded

---

[27] Fitts, 46-47.
[28] Lincoln and Mamiya, 25.
[29] Fitts, 64.

in 1815, the Society's single focus was the evangelization of brothers and sisters on the homeland of Africa. The African Baptist Foreign Missionary Society in 1815 was the forerunner of African missions among African American Baptists. As its founder, Lott Carey assumed leadership in enlisting moral and financial support for African missions among his fellow Afro-American Baptist in the Richmond, Virginia area.[30] When he and Collin Teague left for Africa on January 23, 1821, they carried the hopes, dreams and ambitions of an entire race for the spread of the Gospel in the land of their forefathers.

The kinship the enslaved Africans and newly freed Africans felt for Africa waxed strong and was evidenced in various ways in the African American community. The Late Dr. William J. Harvey, past Executive Secretary of the Foreign Mission Board of the National Baptist Convention USA Inc in his book, *Bridges of Faith Across the Seas* states,

> It is interesting to observe the evidence of the deep sense of relationship American Blacks felt towards

---

[30] Martin, 18.

Africa. Sometimes the word 'African' was made a part of the name of organizations. The church founded by Richard Allen was called the African Methodist Episcopal Church. Later the African Methodist Episcopal Zion Church was founded. Several individual churches use the word in the names they adopted, such as the African Baptist Church. It is clear that such usages reflected a sense of pride on the part of many Blacks in the continent of their heritage. There was, at the same time a deep concern for the people in Africa who were being shamelessly exploited by some of the European power structures.[31]

Dr. Harvey goes further to say that,

"Deep within them [the enslaved African] was a sense of affinity with the land of their ancestors. This was a primary factor in directing their concerns and activities towards spreading the gospel to the land of their forebears."[32]

The fortitude of enslaved Africans in 1815 to envision spreading the Gospel in the land of their forefathers is

---

[31] William J. Harvey, Bridges of Faith Across the Seas: The Story of the Foreign Mission Board National Baptist Convention, USA, Inc., {Philadelphia, PA: The Foreign Mission Board, 1089), 19.

[32] Ibid, 19.

commendable given what they themselves were enduring at the time. Gayraud Wilmore states,

> What is most incredible is that these impoverished and uneducated Black preachers, many with a price still on their heads, had the audacity to think that they could do for Blacks overseas what they could scarcely do for themselves at home. Their aspiration to build self-respecting churches and societies in Africa and the Caribbean outran their capacities at a time when both they and their churches were looked upon with more amusement than respect. But they were not to be daunted by white prejudice. Their concern for taking the gospel to Africa led to the founding of the American Baptist Missionary Convention in 1840 by a group of Black churches in New England and the Middle Atlantic states. It continued for twenty-six years and sent several missionaries to Africa. It was not only evangelism. It was partly a matter of racial pride and self-respect.

Although Sandy Martin maintains that the African American Baptist convention movement was more focused on domestic concerns before emancipation,[33] documentation shows that the determination to share

---

[33] Martin, 16.

the Gospel in Africa remained the focus of the African American Baptist mission.

By the 1870's several African American Baptist Conventions consolidated and merged with the aim of uplifting African Americans through education and evangelization. Martin notes the intentions of the Consolidated American Educational Association, a subsidiary of the Consolidated American Baptist Missionary Convention, was to be "officered and managed principally by colored persons, and laboring for the education and evangelization of their race in the south, in Africa and wherever found unimproved."[34] The African American Baptist Church in its infancy and through the work of newly formed conventions saw African mission as central to its existence. Both Fitts and Martin, in their research note minutes taken at The Triennial Report or Thirty-Seventh Annual Report of the Consolidated American Baptist Missionary Convention highlighting the essential need of African mission by African American Baptists:

---

[34] Martin, 16

The zeal of missionary work in Africa, that characterized our Convention, some fifteen years ago, has all but died out. Our Convention ought to support a missionary in Africa. Indeed, there ought to be a foreign department to the Convention, officered or managed by a Foreign Board, to take entire charge of the Haytian Mission, and to found a Mission in Africa, or cooperate with those already established. We are too great a body, and to deeply concerned in the enlightenment of Africa, to be indifferent in regard to missionary work...

Though of American birth and education, we are nevertheless sons of Africa. God has ordained it... England is circumscribing the continent of Africa, with commercial posts, and acquiring the territory. God signals the intelligent men of our race, to begin to occupy the land lest the African soon became as a wondering Jew, without Judea, and without a Jerusalem."[35]

---

[35] Martin, 17-18 and Fitts, 113.

NATIONAL BAPTIST CONVENTION USA, Inc. FOREIGN MISSION BOARD (FMB)

*A*frican Americans who had served as mission-aries with White mission conventions "were not satisfied with the meager support of African missions on the part of white American Baptists. They were aware of the relationship between black missionary involve-ment and the sociopolitical interests of the Africans. Blacks were more in tune with the heartbeats of their African brothers."[36] African Americans who were sent

---

[36] Fitts, 113-114.

as missionaries by White Baptist conventions returned home eager to get African Americans more involved in African missions. Noted among those sent by a White Baptist Convention is Rev. William W. Colley.

Rev. Colley was sent to West Africa by the Southern Baptist Convention Foreign Mission Board in 1875. He assisted W. J. David, a White Baptist from Mississippi. This arrangement did not work for Colley and as early as 1876 he called for the involvement of African American Baptist in African Missions.[37] Another African American missionary, Solomon Cosby, sent to West Africa in 1878 by African American Baptist Churches of Virginia and jointly supported by the Southern Baptist Convention Foreign Mission Board, similarly registered dissatisfaction with serving in White Convention African Missions. Cosby's dissatisfaction stemmed from working alongside W. J. David, the White Southern Baptist Convention missionary in Nigeria. Martin states that,

> This white missionary envisioned American blacks even on the mission field as playing a

---

[37] Martin, 49.

secondary role to the white missionaries in the evangelization of Africa. Black Christians, on the other hand, saw themselves as God's major instruments to save their African kin, a responsibility they dared not shirk in deference to others.[38]

Upon his return to the USA, after serving under the Southern Baptist Convention Foreign Mission Board, Rev. Colley suggested to African American Baptist church leaders the need to organize a Foreign Mission Convention. On November 24, 1880, 151 African American pastors from 11 states met in Montgomery, Alabama to organize the Baptist Foreign Mission Convention. The official name of the convention was the Baptist Foreign Mission Convention of the United States of America. Rev. Colley served as the first corresponding secretary.[39]

In 1883 Rev. Colley and 5 other missionaries sailed to Liberia to establish work under the Baptist Foreign Mission Convention. These missionaries organized two missions in Bendoo and Jundoo, Liberia. For ten years African American Baptists labored in Liberia under the

---

[38] Martin, 52.
[39] Fitts, 22.

auspices of the Baptist Foreign Mission Convention. By 1893 the last two missionaries were called home to the USA following physical hardship. The work there continued but advanced slowly.[40] During this same period the Southern Baptist Convention Foreign Mission Board "lost momentum in West Africa" and ceased African mission expansion leaving African mission in the hands of the African American Baptist.[41]

The National Baptist Convention USA Inc Foreign Mission Board (FMB) an auxiliary of the National Baptist Convention USA Inc., the largest African American religious body in the United States of America, was the seedling of Baptist Foreign Mission Convention. The National Baptist Convention USA Inc. came into being in 1895 when the Baptist Foreign Mission Convention of the United States of America, the National Education Convention and the American National Baptist Convention consolidated. These three separate African

---

[40] Ibid, 116-117.
[41] Ibid, 115.

American Conventions came together at a time when all three were faltering.

The Baptist Foreign Mission Convention was 14 years old by 1895. It had only one missionary in the field and he was utilizing his own resources. The National Education Convention was one year old and had no school or student and the American National Baptist Convention was eight years old and had no financial resources to support domestic issues. [42]

The resolution approved at the meeting held in 1895 for the consolidation of the three conventions read:

1. That there shall be one national organization of American Baptist.
2. Under this, there shall be a Foreign Mission Board, with authority to plan and execute the foreign mission work according to the spirit and purposes set forth by the Foreign Mission Convention of the United States.
3. There shall be a Board of Education, and also, a Board of Missions to carry into effect the spirit

---

[42] Lewis Garnett Jordan, Negro *Baptist History USA 1750 – 1930* (Nashville, Tennessee: Townsend Press, 1930), 103.

and purpose of the National and the Educational Conventions, respectively.[43]

The purpose of the 1895 consolidation of the three conventions into a national convention was to foster self-expression and mutual benefit. All three conventions had formed individually to bring African American Baptists together and promote unity in the race, both at home and abroad. At home it was observed that, "temperance, education and moral reform stood high on the agenda of many Negro conventions throughout the era – and the influence of such deliberations was carried home by the participants and used to make their communities better places to live."[44] Abroad, the aim of the conventions was to bring the Good News of Jesus to brothers and sisters in the Motherland. "Black Baptist by 1895, despite their organizational problems, had paradoxically moved beyond the local and regional stage in the development of the African missions enterprise and were

---

[43] Jordan, 104.

[44] Howard H. Bell, *A Survey of the Negro Convention Movement 1830-1861* (New York: The Arno Press and the New York Times, 1969), 3.

about to embark upon a truly national effort to redeem the motherland."[45] The goal of the African American Baptist through their newly formed National Baptist Convention was spreading the gospel in Africa because it was the land of their forefathers.[46]

The National Baptist Convention USA Inc. foreign mission ministry was to be carried out through its Foreign Mission Board. At the inception of the National Baptist Convention USA Inc in 1895, the primary focus for missions was Africa. At the Negro Young People's Christian and Educational Congress in 1902, Lewis G. Jordan, second corresponding Secretary of the National Baptist Convention USA Inc Foreign Mission Board (FMB), spoke "on the needs of Africa,"

> If the Negro of America will but feel his responsi-
> bility and under take the evangelization of Africa
> in God's name, unborn millions of Africa's sons

---

[45] Sandy D. Martin, *Black Baptist and African Missions: The Origin of a Movement 1880-1915* (Macon, Georgia: Mercer University Press, 1989), 106.

[46] William J. Harvey III, *Bridges of Faith Across the Seas* (Philadelphia, PA: Foreign Mission Board National Baptist Convention, USA Inc., 1989), 21.

will witness a transformed continent...From
that great black continent can be carved states
and empires, from her cradle will come sons
and daughters to rule and reign in the name of
Christianity. Negroes of America, God calls you
to duty; He calls you to service and He calls
you now.[47]

The National Baptist Convention USA Inc. emerged in
an era of racial tension in the USA marked by "Jim Crow"
segregation legislation, restricted voting rights laws, loss
of political ground after Reconstruction, lynching and the
rise of the Ku Klux Klan. The determination of African
American Baptist persevered and was fueled by their
unwavering commitment to share a Gospel of liberation
that had sustained them in the United States and in which,
they believed, would be the hope of Africa. In spite of significant socio-political obstacles the NBC USA Inc FMB
commissioned 24 Missionaries between the years 1880
to 1915. The majority of these missionaries were South
African. The NBC USA Inc. FMB brought a large number

---

[47] Fitts, 116.

of nationals to the USA to be educated and then to return to southern Africa as missionaries[48]

The National Baptist Convention USA Inc. Foreign Mission Board (FMB) has had a ministry in Southern African for over one hundred years. This ministry has included church planting, the establishment of academic and vocational schools, building clinics and awarding of scholarships for students from pre-school level to graduate studies both on the continent of Africa and in the United States of America. Historically the NBC USA Inc. FMB has been committed to preaching the gospel cross-culturally and helping meet the social needs of the communities in which they have ministered.

---

[48] Martin, 169.

FMB MISSION MINISTRY ADMINISTRATION

*T*he Executive Officers of the FMB, since its inception in 1895 have included the Chairman of the Board, Corresponding Secretary, Treasurer and Recording Secretary. Traditionally, the corresponding secretary position is recognized as the chief administrative role in the organization. However, the title, Corresponding Secretary changed to "Executive Secretary" in the later part of the 1980's. Historically, the accomplishments of the FMB are discussed in relation to the endeavors of the corresponding secretary in setting forth the agenda, goals and objectives of the mission task as that person envisions. As stated earlier, the primary goal of the FMB from its inception was African missions. This goal broadened however, to include mission work in South America, the Caribbean, India and Okinawa.

Rev. L. M. Luke, Corresponding Secretary from September 1895 to December 1895

In 1895 Rev. L.M. Luke was elected the first Corresponding Secretary of the FMB. Rev. Luke's tenure was brief. He died in December of that same year. Rev. Luke had served as Field Secretary of the Baptist Foreign Mission Convention of the United States of America. His election to office was characterized as "earnest."[49]

Rev. Lewis G. Jordan, Corresponding Secretary from February 1896 to September 1921

Rev. Lewis G. Jordan was elected Corresponding Secretary after the death of Rev. Luke. Rev. Jordan laid the foundation for how the FMB would involve itself in African Missions. He took office at a time when African

---

[49] Harvey, 31.

Missions among African American Baptist was at an all time low. He is quoted as having said just after taking office, "there was not a missionary on the field and not a dollar in the treasury."[50] Martin states that, "at the beginning of Jordan's tenure, the Foreign Mission Board faced a number of problems that had plagued its predecessor, the BFMC: heavy financial difficulties, missionaries in Africa inadequately supported, and a lagging interest in foreign mission among Afro-American Baptists.[51] These issues seemed not to deter Rev. Jordan

After the reorganization of the Baptist Foreign Mission Convention under the NBC USA Inc, Rev. Jordan sent 5 missionaries to Africa; other missionaries were sent to West Africa and South America.[52]. Among these missionaries sent to Africa was the Rev. R. A. Jackson, the pioneer of the FMB in South Africa. Jackson's accomplishments in South Africa and the outgrowth of his ministry will be furthered highlighted in the tenure of Rev. James East.

---

[50] Harvey, 37.
[51] Martin, 167.
[52] Fitts, 117.

Rev. Jordan understood the necessity of continual and regular correspondence with the African American National Baptist Churches as well as the African National Baptist churches in Africa. It was under his administration that the *Mission Herald*, the periodical of the FMB, was first published. This periodical became the primary means through which information regarding the work of the FMB was disseminated. The first issue of the *Mission Herald* was published under the title, *Afro-American Mission Herald* in Mid-March of 1896.[53] Today the Mission Herald is published quarterly and is made available to National Baptist Churches in all countries where mission work is being carried out.

Another notable and significant event in Rev. Jordan's administration was his visit to South Africa in 1904, which results in bringing seven young Africans to the United States to be educated. Rev. Jordan traveled to South Africa in 1904 at the request of the South African Church leadership. Their request for his visit was to "assist in improving the organization of the work

---

[53] Harvey, 37.

and to give character and standing before authorities in that country."[54]

> The main purpose of his visit to South Africa was to examine a situation existing between the European Baptists and the native Baptist churches. He found no dealings between these two groups. The white Baptists had begun work in South Africa as early as 1820, whereas the Black Baptist did not begin work there until 1897. The White Baptists were disturbed by some of the practices and certain irregularities carried on by their Black brethren. These practices included men entering the ministry without being ordained and deacons doing work of ministers such as baptizing and administering the Lord's Supper. In reaction to such practices, the white Baptists passed resolutions disassociating themselves from the work carried on by missionaries of the native Baptist conventions sponsored by the Foreign Mission Board.[55]

The mission work in South Africa was established by Rev. R. A. Jackson in 1896. By 1904, Rev. R. A. Jackson, his wife and many of the pioneer missionaries to South Africa had died. The ministry was being carried forward

---

[54] Harvey, 51.
[55] Ibid, 51.

by South African nationals who had been trained and discipled by African American missionaries. The White Baptists in South Africa were in conflict with the Black South African nationals who were carrying on the ministry. Rev. Jordan was able to resolve many of the disagreements between the National Baptist church leaders and the White Baptist church leaders in South Africa. Dr. Harvey recorded the following agreement reached in minutes of the NBC USA Inc in 1904,

> That there may be proper denominational fellowship and cooperation among Baptists of the S. A. Baptist Union, composed of Europeans with some native followers, and Baptists of the South African Baptist Association, composed of colored Baptists, and the Foreign Mission Board of the National Baptist Convention, we, the representative of these bodies, do submit for their consideration, the following:
>
> 1. That we are all anxious to see the truth – bible regeneration, "One Lord, one faith and one baptism," taught among the natives.
> 2. All persons going from the churches of one organization to those of the other must take a letters which will be duly accredited.
> 3. That all the territory possible must be covered and more of the vast army of the lost will be reached

in this country, both organizations will not attempt to work where one can meet the needs in a given locality.

4. That we may have proper leader for the people, we will encourage those feeling called of God to preach the Gospel, to attend school until they attain to the 6th standard before ordination.

5. One in hope, one in doctrine, we will do what we can under God to aid each other in every effort to lift up the millions who now plod on the darkness more dense than light.[56]

When Rev. Jordan returned home from his trip in 1904 he brought back with him seven young Africans. These six men and one woman were educated in the United States with the hope that they would return to Africa as NBC USA Inc FMB missionaries.[57] Martin states that "by 1899 the NBC in particular established a fund to provide for the education of African students in the United States with the understanding that these students would return as missionaries to the African continent.[58] John Chilembwe, the noted Malawian whose image appears

---

[56] Ibid, 52.

[57] Ibid, 58.

[58] Martin, 169.

on Malawian currency, was one of the many Africans educated in the United States through the efforts of the FMB. When he completed his education he returned to his home in Malawi as a FMB missionary.

John B. Chilembwe was brought to the United States by an Englishmen named Joseph Booth, in 1897. Soon after his arrival in the country Chilembwe was introduced to Rev. Lewis G. Jordan, Corresponding Secretary of the FMB. Rev. Jordan enrolled Chilembwe at the Virginia Theological Seminary and College in Lynchburg, Virginia in 1898. After Chilembwe completed his education in the United States and was ordained as a Baptist minister he returned to his home in Malawi which was then called Nyasaland, British Central Africa in 1899.[59] Chilembwe opened the Providence Industrial Mission (PIM) in Chiradzulu, Malawi in 1900. John Chilembwe led a resistance against the British government in 1915. As a result of this resistance Providence Industrial Mission was attacked and destroyed by British colonist, and Chilembwe was killed. It was thought that the Providence

---

[59] Fitts, 137.

Industrial Mission would never reopen.[60] In 1926, however, a former student of Chilembwe who had studied in the United States returned to Malawi to reopen PIM. Dr. Daniel S. Malekebu, who had assisted Chilembwe in the development of PIM when he was young boy, returned to Malawi to see that the mission continued.

Rev. Jordan laid a firm foundation for the future growth of the NBC USA Inc FMB. Under his administration the FMB commenced the publication of the Mission Herald. He saw the necessity of traveling to the mission fields to see first hand the conditions of the missionaries and their needs. He also established the tradition of education for mission leaders both at home and abroad. Under Rev. Jordan's leadership African missions was expanded into South Africa, Malawi and Nigeria and gained firmer footing in Liberia. In September 1921 Rev. Lewis G. Jordan resigned as corresponding Secretary of the NBC USA Inc FMB due to ill health. He was then named Corresponding Secretary emeritus. He continued

---

[60]Harvey, 209.

his involvement with the FMB serving on several committees. Rev. Jordan died February 25, 1939.

Rev. James E. East, Corresponding Secretary from September 1921-October 1934

Rev. James E. East was elected Corresponding Secretary after the resignation of Rev. Lewis G. Jordon in September 1921. He is the only corresponding secretary in FMB history to have had experience in the mission field. Rev. East and his wife Lucinda served in South Africa from 1909 to 1920. While in South Africa Rev. East, and his wife, reopened the mission that was started by Rev. J. I. Buchanan.

Following the deaths of Rev. Buchanan and his wife, who began their mission work with Rev. R. A. Jackson in Cape Town, South Africa in 1897, the mission work in South Africa went unmonitored. Rev. Buchanan and his wife while in South Africa, spent most of their time in the township of Middledrift in the former Transkei (a Black South African Homeland under the apartheid government) where Rev. Buchanan was instrumental in ordaining preachers and opening a vocational school for carpentry and masonry. Rev. Buchanan also helped to organize the convention of National Baptist church leaders in South Africa.[61] Rev. James East reopened the work in Middledrift in 1910.

Rev. East served as corresponding secretary for 13 years. Drawing on his missionary experience in South Africa, Rev. East took the FMB in new directions. Through his leadership the FMB began medical mission ministry. In 1926, he opened the Carrie V. Dyer Hospital in Liberia. He also commissioned Dr. Daniel Malekebu to reopen the PIM in Malawi where the first medical mission was started.

Dr. Malekebu received medical training at Meharry Medical College in Nashville, Tennessee. Once he completed his training he first returned to Malawi with the help of the Lott Carey Foreign Mission Convention, but later applied for commission with the FMB. Dr. Malekebu was instrumental in establishing the medical mission work in Malawi. It was because of his pioneering work in medical mission at the Providence Industrial Mission that by 1974

---

[61] Harvey, 43.

a clinic was opened at PIM specializing in pre-natal care. The Clinic is still in operation today.

During his administration Rev. East also had to deal with complications of sending African American missionaries to Africa. European nations objected to the commissioning of African American missionaries because they believed that African Americans would influence the African with ideas of independence and Nationalism.[62] Robert Vinson, in an article entitled, "Citizenship Over Race?: African Americans in American-South African Diplomacy, 1890-1925," discusses how South Africans associated African Americans with subversive actions of Black South Africans at the time of the rise of Ethiopianism, which was the term used to denote the Black South African independence church movement.[63] Rev. East stated in minutes from the NBC USA Inc in 1925 that:

---

[62] Fitts, 120-121.

[63] Robert Vinson, "Citizenship Over Race?: African Americans in American –South African Diplomacy, 1890-1925." http://www.historycooperative.org/journals/whc/2.1/vinson.html., (accessed November 20, 2007).

Now, however, the governments have notified their consuls representing them in this country not to vise (sic) passports, and have also notified steamship companies not to sell tickets to any colored missionaries wishing to come to parts of Africa unless they produce a permit from such countries. Now when we go to get the permit, the next question that arises is, "Is there a white man at the head of the Society under which your missionaries wish to come out? As soon as we say, "No," the permit is denied us. Of course, the reasons they give for this are that Negro missionaries are not practical, that they are agitators and they stir up the natives to rebellion against the respective Europeans in charge of them.[64]

Nevertheless, Rev. East did not allow these attitudes to deter him. When African Americans were prevented from being sent to Africa as missionaries, especially in South Africa during the years 1921 to 1960, Rev. East placed nationals in charge of the mission work. For example, in South Africa Rev. East appointed Rev. E. B. P. Koti, a South African, as supervisor over South African mission work.[65] Rev. Koti was ordained by Rev. R. A. Jackson in

---

[64] Harvey, 77-78.
[65] Fitts, 141.

1897. He traveled to the United States several times under Rev. L. G. Jordan's administration to become familiar with the leadership of the National Baptist Convention. Rev. Koti organized the African United National Baptist Churches Assembly in South Africa and was first to compile the African United National Baptist Hymnal entitled, *Incwadi Ya-muculo*.[66]

Rev. East died on October 2, 1934. He brought to the position of corresponding secretary firsthand knowledge and experience as a missionary in Africa. These qualities combined with his commitment to the "Great Commission" made him an exceptional leader. Following his death the NBC USA Inc. appointed Rev. C. C. Adams as interim corresponding secretary from October 1934 to December 1934. In December the NBC USA Inc. appointed Rev. Joseph H. Jackson, Corresponding Secretary.

---

[66] Jones, 93, 97.

Rev. Joseph H. Jackson, Corresponding Secretary from December 1934 to September 1941

Rev. Joseph Jackson became Corresponding Secretary during the "Great Depression." Given the economic conditions of the United States at this time, incredibly, the mission work of the FMB continued. Rev. Jackson was able to set up several fundraising ventures that kept the mission work afloat. He is credited with establishing policies for operating budgets at mission stations which increased the financial efficiency of the FMB. Under his administration new mission work was opened in South America, the Caribbean, and Japan.[67]

World War II presented the greatest challenge for Rev. Jackson and the FMB. Needless to say, the war prevented missionary travel to mission fields and created transportation hazards for those returning home on furlough. In spite of these difficulties, ten men and women were sent out by the FMB under Jackson's leadership.[68] Rev. Jackson resigned from the office of corresponding

---

[67] Harvey, 125-127.
[68] Ibid, 136.

secretary in 1941 to pastor the Olivet Baptist Church in Chicago, Illinois. Rev. Dr. C. C. Adams succeeded Rev. Jackson as Corresponding Secretary.

Rev. Dr. C. C. Adams, Corresponding Secretary from September 1941-September 1961

Rev. Dr. Adams took leadership of the FMB at the beginning of World War II. Because the war effort at home continued to create financial strain for the FMB, Dr. Adams instituted several fundraising programs that fostered financial support and interest in foreign missions. One of his fundraising programs was an Annual Christmas Drive held in each state. The Christmas Drive was designed to create an atmosphere for not only raising funds for the mission work of the FMB, but also to provided educational opportunities in mission ministry for pastors and church leaders. In 1943 the first Annual Christmas Drives held in 43 States raised a combined total of $100,000. Dr. Adams also initiated a 10 year program to raise $2 million between the years 1944-1954. In the fiscal year 1945-1946 the FMB had raised $200,000.[69]

By 1950 interest and support of missions was on an increase. That year the FMB sponsored the first of many preaching team visits to Africa. Ten pastors from across the United States went on this first FMB sponsored visit to Africa. These visits were designed to give pastors first-hand experience in African missions.

Dr. Adams made several trips to Africa during his tenure. Notable are his 1945 trip to Liberia and his 1947 trip to South Africa. On both occasions he evidenced the growth of the mission ministry in the respective countries and recognized the need to appoint regional supervisors to coordinate the ministry. Rev. John B. Falconer, a former chaplain in the United States Army, was assigned supervisor of Liberia and Dr. Daniel Malekebu, who was serving as supervisor in Malawi, was appointed to also supervise South Africa.

Like his predecessor, Dr. Adams opened mission work outside of Africa. Under his administration a mission post

---

[69] Harvey, 150-154.

was opened in Okinawa in 1947. In conjunction with the National Baptist Convention of America unincorporated, the FMB provided a salary for one mission worker.[70]

Dr. Adams served as corresponding secretary during the National Baptist's most fractious period. The division started when a group of National Baptist pastors challenged now President Rev. J.H. Jackson's ruling that the convention's constitutional amendment to limit the president's term to four years was invalid because it was procedurally incorrect. The court ruled in Jackson's favor. As a result, the ten pastors who had challenged Jackson's decision were expelled from the Convention.[71]

Jackson was not supportive of the civil rights movement. He condemned the movement as "injurious to the cause of racial harmony."[72] This did not sit well with prominent National Baptist pastors such as Martin Luther King Jr., Ralph Abernathy, Gardner C. Taylor and Benjamin Mays, who were also major civil rights

---

[70] Harvey, 163.
[71] Lincoln and Mamiya, 36.
[72] Ibid, 36.

leaders. The pastors' expulsions, Jackson's autocratic rule, along with Jackson's opposition to the civil rights movement were seeds that caused greater division among the National Baptist.

In 1960 Jackson's opponents supported Rev. Gardner C. Taylor as president of the Convention. However, the nominating committee unanimously presented Jackson's name. Jackson was elected by voice vote. The Taylor supporters demanded a roll call by states. Before considering the procedure, the Convention was adjourned. Even so, the delegates remained, an election was conducted and Taylor won. This election caused much havoc and prevented the Convention from moving forward. A year later in Kansas City, Missouri, the court supervised the election of the Convention's president. Jackson won the election. Convention officers who supported Taylor were stripped of their positions. Dr. Adams was included in this group. He was the first corresponding secretary of the FMB to be removed from office. Dr. William J. Harvey III was appointed to replace Dr. Adams.

*Rev. Dr. William J. Harvey III, Corresponding Secretary
(Executive Secretary) from September 1961 to
September 2001*

Dr. William J. Harvey III took over as Corresponding
Secretary during a turbulent time in NBC USA Inc. history. His appointment to the position of corresponding
secretary went uncontested, however the officers that had
been removed from office in the NBC USA Inc. established the Progressive National Baptist Convention. The
Foreign Mission Bureau carried out the mission ministry
of the newly formed convention. Several indigenous missionaries who had begun service under the leadership of
Dr. C. C. Adams opted to remain under his leadership
and severed their relationships with the NBC USA Inc.
FMB. Consequently, the NBC USA Inc. FMB lost mission work in Nigeria.

However, Dr. Harvey gained the much needed support to recover from the fallout of the 1960 elections. By
1962 he made his first trip to Liberia. On this trip the
Liberian government requested to purchase the Carrie
Dyer Memorial Hospital which was built in 1926. A
settlement was made. The Liberian government paid

$350,000 for the hospital to be paid over a 10 year period. The money from the sale was used for health services conducted at the Bendoo and Suehn Missions.[73]

By 1973 Dr. Harvey had successfully organized three preaching team trips to the mission fields in Africa. Thereafter he made preaching team and inspection tour trips to the mission fields in Africa every other year. His last trip with the preaching teams was in 1993. In 1984 Dr. Harvey led a delegation of members of the Women's Auxiliary of the NBC USA Inc to Malawi for the dedication of the S. Willie Layton Memorial Hospital which is in operation today.

In 1971 the NBC USA Inc. FMB opened mission work in the Kingdom of Swaziland. The supervisor in southern Africa at the time was Rev. E. D. Ngubeni. Rev. Ngubeni had studied in the United States and returned to South Africa in 1962. Dr. Harvey saw great promise in Rev. Ngubeni. In 1969 Rev. Ngubeni approached Dr. Harvey requesting that the FMB begin mission work in the Kingdom of Swaziland. Rev. Elias and Doreen Pudule,

---

[73] Harvey, 201.

a South African couple who were educated in the United States relocated to Swaziland to begin the ministry. While Rev. Pudule did church planting, Doreen Pudule began pioneering work in Pre-School education. She organized and supervised the first Pre-school in the Kingdom of Swaziland. Prior to the opening of the National Baptist Church Pre-School the Kingdom of Swaziland had no pre-school education. The ministry in Swaziland grew as churches were planted. A second pre-school was opened in the town of Nhlangano at the National Baptist Church in Nhlangano.[74]

Dr. Harvey also instituted employment policies for all missionaries both indigenous and those from the United States. Health care benefits and life insurance policies were put in place as well as a plan to steadily increase missionary salaries. Over 50 missionaries were commissioned to serve in Africa, the Caribbean, and Nicaragua during Dr. Harvey's tenure. This author was commissioned in 1991 and served 8 years in the Kingdom of

---

[74] Interview with Rev. Elias Pudule, November 2006.

Swaziland and South Africa under the leadership of Dr. Harvey.

Dr. Harvey resigned from office in September 2001 for health reasons. He served as corresponding secretary for 41 years. Upon his retirement, the Annual Foreign Mission Dinner held at the Annual National Baptist Convention was named after him. Dr. Charles Walker was appointed Executive Secretary in January 2002 at the Winter Board meeting held in Nashville, Tennessee. In September 2006 Dr. Harvey died of a stroke while attending the Annual National Baptist Convention in Dallas, Texas.

Dr. Charles Walker, Executive Secretary from January 2002 to June 2003

Dr. Charles Walker served as Chairman of the Foreign Mission Board for 19 years before being appointed interim Executive Secretary at the January National Baptist Convention USA Inc Mid-Winter Board Meeting held in Nashville, Tennessee. The FMB recommended at the meeting to suspend the search for a successor to Dr. William J. Harvey because they felt it necessary to "redefine and refocus our mission mandate in the new millennium." Dr. Walker was chosen to give leadership through this transition period. [75]

Before being named Chairman of the Foreign Mission Board, Dr. Walker as a member of the Board, made a heroic trip to Liberia in 1980 at the height of revolution following the assassination of President William R. Tolbert. In notes from the 1980 July-August issues of the Mission Herald, cited in *Bridges of Faith Across the Seas*, Dr. Harvey tells how Dr. Walker was physically accosted by uniformed Liberian soldiers and made to striped to his underwear before intervention by soldiers from the executive mansion.[76] Dr. Walker also led several of the Preaching/Inspection Team Tours in the later years of Dr. Harvey's administration due to Dr. Harvey's failing health. Because of his close working relationship with Dr. Harvey, Dr. Walker was the logical choice

---

[75] Information taken from a letter written to this author thanking her for her interest in the position of Executive Secretary of the FMB dated February 8, 2002.

[76] Harvey, 305.

for corresponding secretary after Dr. William J. Harvey' resignation.

Though Dr. Walker served as interim Executive Secretary for less than two years, he was instrumental in initiating FMB involvement in addressing HIV/AIDS in southern Africa. In his Vision Plan for the Foreign Mission Board published in the 2002 July-August issue of the Mission Herald, Dr. Walker recommended building a hospital in Zambia "to curb AIDS and bring hope to the people of Zambia."[77] The recommendation for a hospital was not carried out in Zambia; however, Dr. Walker endorsed and recommended to the National Baptist Convention USA Inc. FMB a proposal submitted by Missionary Debra Townes stationed in the Kingdom of Swaziland for the construction of a clinic in Swaziland. In July 2004 the clinic in Swaziland was officially opened by Dr. William Shaw, President of the National Baptist Convention USA Inc. The National Baptist Mission Clinic

---

[77] Reverend Dr. Charles Walker, "The Vision Plan for the Foreign Mission board of the N.B.C., USA, Inc.," Mission Herald, July/August 2002, 3-5.

in the Kingdom of Swaziland provides HIV/AIDS testing and counseling, general health care and immunizations.

Also included in Dr. Walker's Vision Plan were recommendations for the recruitment and training of missionaries which would mean securing a full-time Director of Recruitment and Training whose function would be to "seek qualified candidates for the mission field." Dr. Walker further recommended that training for all missionaries include:

- Knowledge of the history of the country (area and village) in which they serve
- Knowledge of the particular cultural traditions (i.e., art, literature, and music)
- Understanding of tribal relationships
- Understanding Colonial History
- Intensive language training in the local language
- Employment of approximately 10 part-time teachers from the country where missionaries will serve for the purposes of culture interpretation[78]

---

[78] Ibid, 3.

Dr. Walker resigned as interim Executive Secretary in June 2003. Following his resignation the Administration of the FMB was given to a Management Team. The Management Team was comprised of the Chairman of the FMB Rev. William B. Moore, the Vice-Chairman of the FMB Rev. Dr. J. Wendell Mapson, Jr. and two members of the Executive Committee Rev. James Moore, Sr. and Rev. Albert G. Davis. The Management Team provided oversight of the day to day operations of the Foreign Mission Board's work. At the Annual Session of the National Baptist Convention USA Inc. held in Philadelphia, Pennsylvania September 3-7, 2007, Rev. Dr. Joe Albert Bush was named Executive Secretary of the National Baptist Convention USA Inc Foreign Mission Board.

Rev. Dr. Joe Albert Bush resigned from the position of Executive Secretary in September 2011. Rev. Nicolas Richards succeeded Rev. Dr. Joe Albert Bush as Executive Secretary. The mission ministry accomplishments of both Rev. Dr. Bush and Rev. Richards are yet to be documented.

CONCLUSION

The mission ministry of the National Baptist Convention USA, Inc. Foreign Mission Board (FMB) from its conception has focused on spreading the Gospel of Jesus Christ particularly on the continent of Africa. Over the years the mission ministry expanded to include nations in the western hemisphere and Asia. Today, once again the mission ministry focus of the FMB is on the continent of Africa. Mission work continues in South Africa, Swaziland, Liberia, Guinea, Malawi and Lesotho. In future discussions I hope to highlight the mission ministry of the FMB in the 21st century as nationals resume in many cases leadership positions and provide ministry training in their respective countries where once African American mission workers assumed these roles.

The call of the Great Commission of Jesus Christ to go into all the world and make disciples is still the call to all men and women of faith. African American Baptists have heeded the call and in the past and show evidence of continued ministry to Jesus Christ whether home or abroad.

References

African American Baptist in Mission:

A Historical Guide

Fitts, Leroy. *A History of Black Baptists*. Nashville
Tennessee: Boardman Press, 1985.

_____. *Lott Carey: First Black Missionary to Africa*.
Valley Forge, PA: Judson Press, 1982.

Harvey, William J. *Bridges of Faith Across the Seas: The
Story of the Foreign Mission Board National Baptist
Convention, USA Inc*. Philadelphia, PA: The Foreign
Mission Board, 1989.

Jones, Roxanne. "African American Religious Influence
in South Africa: The Case of the Baptist Church."
Journal of Constructive Theology 4 no.2 (December
1998): 87-99.

Lincoln, C. Eric and Lwarence H. Mamiya. *The Black Church in the African American Experience*. Durham and London: Duke University Press, 1990.

Martin, Sandy D. *Black Baptist and Africa Missions: The Origins of a Movement 1880-1925*. Macon, Georgia: Mercer University Press, 1989.

_____. "Spelman's Emma B. Delaney and the African Mission," *Journal of Religious Thought*. 41: 22-37, 1984-1985.

Raboteau, Albert J. *Slave Religion: The "Invisible Institution" in the Antebellum South*. Oxford: Oxford University Press, 1978.

Scherer, Lester B. "Black Baptist in the United States: Research and Resources," *American Baptist Quarterly* 1 no.1 (October 1982):69-73.

Shepperson, George and Thomas Price. *Independent African: John "Chilembwe and the Origins, Settings and significance of the Nyasaland Native Rising of 1915*. Edinburgh, Scotland: Edinburgh University Press, 1958.

Walston, Vaughn J. and Robert J. Stevens, eds. *African-American Experience in World Mission: A Call*

Beyond Community. Pasadena, California: William Carey Library, 2002.

Wilmore, Gayraud S. "Black Americans in Mission: Setting the Record Straight," *International Bulletin of Missionary Research* (July 1986): 98-102.

Websites

Vinson, Robert. "Citizenship Over Race?: African-Americans in American –SouthAfrican Diplomacy,1890-1925."
http://www.historycooperative.org/journals/whc/2.1/vinson.html., (accessed November 20, 2007).

About the Author:

*R*ev. Dr. Roxanne Jones Booth serves along-side her husband, the Rev. Antonio Booth, as Co-Pastor of the Riverview Missionary Baptist Church in Coeymans, NY. She is a three-time graduate of Howard University having received the degrees of Bachelor of Arts, Master of Arts in Religious Studies and the Master of Divinity. She is also a graduate of Gordon-Conwell Theological Seminary having received the Doctor of Ministry degree specializing in Missions and Cross-Cultural Studies.

Currently, Rev. Dr. Booth is also an Adjunct Professor at the State University of New York at Albany in the College of Arts and Sciences Department of Africana

Studies lecturing in African and African American Religion.

Utilizing her 10 years missions experience as a mission worker with the National Baptist Convention USA Inc. Foreign Mission Board in the Kingdom of Swaziland and South Africa and her doctoral training in missions and cross-cultural studies, Rev. Dr. Booth facilitates mission ministry training workshops throughout the United States and is an instructor in the mission studies program of the Lott Carey Baptist Foreign Mission Convention.

Additionally, since becoming Co-Pastor at Riverview in 2010, Rev. Dr. Booth coordinates annual short-term mission trips to Southern Africa through the Riverview Missionary Baptist Church Short-term Mission Trip Ministry. Rev. Dr. Booth is also a life-time member of Delta Sigma Theta Sorority, Inc. and serves as Chapter Historian for the Albany, NY Alumnae Chapter.

CPSIA information can be obtained
at www.ICGtesting.com
Printed in the USA
FFOW05n1120260515